© 2024 by FAISAL JAMIL. All rights reserved.

Title: "The Golden Gateways: Understanding the UAE Golden Visa"

This book, along with its contents encompassing text, illustrations, images, diagrams, and other creative elements, is the exclusive property of FAISAL JAMIL and is safeguarded by copyright law.

FAISAL JAMIL asserts full ownership and retains all rights to this book. No part of this publication may be reproduced, distributed, or transmitted in any form or by any means, such as photocopying, recording, or electronic methods, without prior written consent from the copyright holder. Brief quotations in critical reviews and certain noncommercial uses permitted by copyright law are exceptions.

This copyright notice applies to all editions, formats, and translations of the book, whether in print, digital, or any other medium or technology existing now or developed in the future. Unauthorized use or infringement may result in legal action and pursuit of remedies under applicable copyright laws.

While efforts have been made to ensure accuracy and reliability, FAISAL JAMIL does not guarantee the completeness or suitability of the information. Readers are responsible for evaluating and using the content judiciously.

FAISAL JAMIL reserves the right to make changes, updates, or corrections to the book without prior notice. Inclusion of third-party materials or references does not imply endorsement or affiliation unless used under fair use principles or with proper permissions and attributions.

For permissions, inquiries, or requests regarding the book's use, please contact FAISAL JAMIL through official channels listed on their Amazon author page or provided email address.

This comprehensive copyright notice serves to protect FAISAL JAMIL'S intellectual property rights, maintain content control, and inform users about associated restrictions and permissions.

Warm regards,

FAISAL JAMIL

For your feedback and reviews:

http://www.amazon.com/author/faisal.jamil

Email: faisaljamilauthor@gmail.com

About the author

Certainly! Faisal Jamil is a multifaceted individual with a diverse set of skills and experiences. With a strong foundation in computer knowledge since childhood, he has developed a deep understanding of technology that informs his work as a content writer. Faisal also possesses digital skills, which further enhance his abilities in various digital platforms and technologies.

Beyond his professional endeavors, Faisal Jamil has also excelled in the martial arts, particularly Shotokan Karate, where he achieved the prestigious rank of first Dan black belt. This achievement speaks to his dedication, discipline, and commitment to personal growth and mastery.

In his professional life, Faisal Jamil has carved out a successful career in sales management within the Fast Moving Consumer Goods (FMCG) sector. His roles in various FMCG companies have honed his skills in strategic planning, team leadership, and business development. Faisal's ability to drive sales and achieve targets has been instrumental in his career progression, showcasing his talent for identifying opportunities and delivering results.

Faisal Jamil is also deeply interested in business investment strategies, planning, and execution. His understanding of these areas has been key to his success in the business world, allowing him to make informed decisions and implement effective strategies. His ability to navigate the complexities of investment planning and execution has set him apart as a strategic thinker and a valuable asset in any business endeavor.

Overall, Faisal Jamil is a dynamic individual who combines his passion for technology, martial arts, sales management, digital skills, and business investment strategies to achieve success in diverse fields. His journey is a testament to his versatility, resilience, and continuous pursuit of excellence.

Yours Sincerely

FAISAL JAMIL

For your feedback and reviews:

https://www.amazon.com/author/faisal.jamil

Email: faisaljamilauthor@gmail.com

THE GOLDEN GATEWAYS UNDERSTANDING THE UAE GOLDEN VISA

Introduction

In recent years, the United Arab Emirates (UAE) has emerged as a global hub for business, innovation, and lifestyle. One of the key initiatives driving this transformation is the UAE Golden Visa program, which offers long-term residency permits to eligible individuals. In 2022, the program witnessed a significant surge, with around 80,000 Golden Visas issued across all categories, marking a 68% increase from the previous year. This book delves into the details of the UAE Golden Visa program, its impact, and the opportunities it presents for individuals and the UAE alike.

Table of Content

Preface

Chapter 1: The Evolution of the UAE Golden Visa

Chapter 2: Recent Changes and Amendments

Chapter 3: Eligibility and Requirements for the Golden Visa

Chapter 4: Benefits of the Golden Visa

Chapter 5: Impact on Business and Investment

Chapter 6: Cultural and Social Integration

Chapter 7: Future Prospects and Challenges

Conclusion

Preface

The United Arab Emirates (UAE) has emerged as a beacon of opportunity, attracting individuals from around the world with its dynamic economy, vibrant culture, and unparalleled quality of life. At the heart of this allure is the UAE's Golden Visa program, a groundbreaking initiative that offers long-term residency to investors, entrepreneurs, and talented professionals seeking to make the UAE their home.

"The Golden Gateways: Understanding the UAE Golden Visa" is a comprehensive guide that explores the intricacies of this transformative program. From its inception to its evolution, this book provides a detailed examination of how the Golden Visa program has shaped the UAE's economic and social landscape.

In these pages, readers will discover the historical background of the Golden Visa program and its significance in the context of the UAE's vision for the future. They will learn about the eligibility criteria and application process, gaining insights into the specific requirements for each category of applicant.

The book also delves into the recent changes and amendments to the Golden Visa program, including the introduction of new residency options and the ability for visa holders to sponsor their family members and domestic help. These changes have not only expanded the program's reach but have also made it more attractive and accessible to a diverse range of individuals.

Furthermore, "The Golden Gateways" explores the cultural and social integration of Golden Visa holders in the UAE, highlighting the country's commitment to diversity and inclusivity. It also discusses the economic impact of the Golden Visa program, showcasing how it has contributed to the UAE's GDP growth and economic diversification.

As we embark on this journey through the world of the UAE Golden Visa, I invite you to join me in exploring the opportunities and challenges of this transformative program. Whether you are an investor, entrepreneur, or simply curious about the UAE's Golden Visa program, this book offers a comprehensive and insightful guide to understanding one of the most innovative residency programs in the world.

Chapter 1

The Evolution of the UAE Golden Visa

I: Historical Background and the Inception of the Golden Visa Program

The concept of the Golden Visa, also known as the UAE Long-Term Residency Visa, was introduced in the United Arab Emirates (UAE) in 2019. The program was launched as part of the UAE government's efforts to attract high net worth individuals, investors, and talented professionals to the country. The program came at a time when the UAE was seeking to diversify its economy and reduce its reliance on oil revenue, which had been the mainstay of the country's economy for many years.

The UAE has long been known for its business-friendly environment, with zero income tax and a strategic location that serves as a gateway between East and West. These factors have made the UAE an attractive destination for businesses and investors from around the world. However, the introduction of the Golden Visa program aimed to further enhance the country's appeal by offering long-term residency permits to eligible individuals.

The Golden Visa program was designed to provide stability and security to individuals and their families, allowing them to live, work, and study in the UAE without the need for frequent renewals or a national sponsor. The program offers residency permits that are valid for 5-10 years, depending on the category of the applicant, and can be renewed automatically.

Overall, the Golden Visa program has been instrumental in attracting high net worth individuals, investors, and talented professionals to the UAE, helping to diversify the country's economy and position it as a global hub for business and innovation. As the program continues to evolve, it is expected to play an increasingly important role in shaping the future of the UAE.

II: Overview of the Eligibility Criteria and Application Process

The Golden Visa program in the UAE is open to a wide range of individuals, including investors, entrepreneurs, specialized talents, researchers, and students. Each category has its own set of eligibility criteria, but in general, applicants must meet certain financial, professional, and legal requirements to qualify for the visa.

For investors, the minimum investment required is AED 2 million, which can be in the form of investment funds, commercial or industrial investments with a specified minimum annual turnover, or ownership of a company with a minimum annual revenue. Entrepreneurs, on the other hand, must be partners in a company registered in the UAE under the SME category and have a minimum annual revenue of AED 1 million.

Specialized talents, including doctors, scientists, artists, and researchers, must demonstrate exceptional skills and qualifications in their respective fields. They may also need to provide evidence of their achievements and contributions to their field.

Students who wish to apply for the Golden Visa must have a certain level of academic achievement and be enrolled in a recognized educational institution in the UAE. They may also need to provide proof of their enrollment and academic standing.

The application process for the Golden Visa is relatively straightforward, requiring applicants to submit the necessary documents and undergo a thorough background check. Some of the documents that may be required include:

A: Passport copy

B: Proof of investment or ownership of a company

C: Academic certificates and transcripts

D: Proof of enrollment in a recognized educational

institution (for students)

E: Professional certificates and qualifications

(for specialized talents)

F: Any other documents requested by the authorities

Once the application is submitted, it will be reviewed by the relevant authorities, and if approved, the applicant will be issued a Golden Visa. The visa is typically valid for 5-10 years, depending on the category of the applicant, and can be renewed automatically as long as the applicant continues to meet the eligibility criteria.

III: Comparison with Other Residency Programs Around the World

The UAE Golden Visa program is unique in its scope and benefits compared to other residency programs around the world. While many countries offer residency programs for investors and skilled professionals, the UAE's program stands out for several reasons.

One of the key differences is the duration of the Golden Visa. Unlike many other residency programs that offer temporary or short-term residency permits, the UAE's program allows individuals to reside in the country for extended periods, ranging from 5 to 10 years, depending on the category of the applicant. This provides individuals and their families with long-term stability and security, eliminating the need for frequent renewals and providing a sense of permanence in the country.

Another key difference is the flexibility and freedom offered by the Golden Visa program. Unlike some residency programs that require individuals to have a national sponsor or restrict their ability to work or study, the UAE's program allows Golden Visa holders to live, work, and study in the country without the need for a sponsor. This flexibility has made the program highly attractive to individuals seeking a stable and prosperous future in the UAE.

Additionally, the UAE Golden Visa program offers a range of benefits and incentives to its holders. These include access to various discounts on services and amenities, as well as the ability to sponsor family members and domestic help.

These benefits, combined with the program's long duration and flexibility, have made the UAE Golden Visa program one of the most sought-after residency programs in the world.

Overall, the UAE Golden Visa program represents a significant evolution in the country's approach to residency and immigration. By offering long-term residency permits with a range of benefits and incentives, the program has positioned the UAE as a global leader in attracting talent and investment, and has helped to diversify the country's economy and enhance its reputation as a business-friendly destination.

Chapter 2
Recent Changes and Amendments

I: Introduction of Different Types of Residency Options and Entry Visas

The UAE government has recently introduced several changes and amendments to the Golden Visa program, aimed at enhancing its appeal and flexibility for applicants. One of the key changes is the introduction of different types of residency options and entry visas, providing more choices for individuals seeking to live and work in the UAE.

These new options include long-term residency permits for investors, entrepreneurs, specialized talents, researchers, students, and humanitarian pioneers. Each category has its own set of eligibility criteria and benefits, allowing individuals to choose the option that best suits their needs and circumstances.

A: Investors: Investors can apply for a Golden Visa by making a minimum investment of AED 2 million in the UAE. This investment can be in the form of investment funds, commercial or industrial investments, or ownership of a company with a minimum annual revenue.

B: Entrepreneurs: Entrepreneurs can apply for a Golden Visa if they are partners in a company registered in the UAE under the SME category and have a minimum annual revenue of AED 1 million.

C: Specialized Talents: Specialized talents, including doctors, scientists, artists, and researchers, can apply for a Golden Visa if they can demonstrate exceptional skills and qualifications in their respective fields.

D: Students: Students who are enrolled in a recognized educational institution in the UAE can apply for a Golden Visa. They must meet certain academic achievement criteria and provide proof of their enrollment.

E: Humanitarian Pioneers: UAE has always been impactful with its humanitarian initiatives and their empowered works and it can become a second home to these individuals.

Each of these categories has its own set of benefits, including the ability to live, work, and study in the UAE without the need for a national sponsor. Additionally, Golden Visa holders can enjoy various discounts and incentives offered by the UAE government and private sector entities.

Overall, the introduction of these new residency options and entry visas has made the UAE Golden Visa program more inclusive and attractive to a wider range of individuals, further enhancing the country's appeal as a global destination for talent and investment.

II: Amendments Easing Eligibility Criteria and Expanding Beneficiary Categories

In addition to introducing new residency options, the UAE government has also made amendments to the Golden Visa program to ease eligibility criteria and expand beneficiary categories. These changes have made it easier for a wider range of individuals to qualify for the Golden Visa, increasing the program's attractiveness to potential applicants.

One significant amendment is the ability for Golden Visa holders to sponsor their family members and domestic help. This change has provided greater flexibility and support for visa holders, allowing them to bring their families to the UAE to live with them. This has been particularly beneficial for expatriates who wish to have their families with them while they work or study in the UAE.

The amendments have also expanded the categories of beneficiaries eligible for the Golden Visa. In addition to investors, entrepreneurs, specialized talents, researchers, students, and humanitarian pioneers, the program now includes categories such as outstanding students, graduates, and frontline heroes. This expansion has opened up the program to a wider range of individuals, further increasing its appeal.

Overall, the amendments to the Golden Visa program have made it more accessible and attractive to individuals seeking to live and work in the UAE. By easing eligibility criteria and expanding beneficiary categories, the UAE government has demonstrated its commitment to attracting top talent and investment to the country, further enhancing its reputation as a global hub for business and innovation.

III: Ability for Visa Holders to Sponsor Family Members and Domestic Help

One of the most significant changes to the Golden Visa program is the ability for visa holders to sponsor their family members and domestic help. This change has been welcomed by many expatriates, as it allows them to bring their loved ones to live with them in the UAE without the need for a separate sponsorship.

Under the new rules, Golden Visa holders can sponsor their spouses, children, and parents, as well as domestic workers such as maids, drivers, and nannies. This has made it easier for families to stay together and has increased the appeal of the Golden Visa program for individuals with family members who wish to join them in the UAE.

The ability to sponsor family members and domestic help has also provided greater support and assistance to Golden Visa holders. Family members can now accompany visa holders to the UAE and live with them, providing them with a sense of security and comfort. Additionally, the ability to sponsor domestic help has made it easier for visa holders to manage their household affairs and maintain a work-life balance.

Overall, the recent changes and amendments to the Golden Visa program have made it more attractive and accessible to a wider range of individuals. By introducing new residency options, easing eligibility criteria, and allowing visa holders to sponsor their family members and domestic help, the UAE government has demonstrated its commitment to enhancing the program and ensuring its continued success.

Chapter 3

Eligibility and Requirements for the Golden Visa

I: Detailed Explanation of Who is Eligible for the Golden Visa

The Golden Visa program in the UAE is designed to attract high net worth individuals, investors, entrepreneurs, specialized talents, students, and researchers to live and work in the country. The eligibility criteria vary depending on the category of the applicant, but in general, individuals must meet certain financial, professional, and legal requirements to qualify for the visa.

A: Investors: To qualify for the Golden Visa as an investor, individuals must have a minimum investment of AED 2 million in the UAE. This investment can be in the form of investment funds, commercial or industrial investments, or ownership of a company with a specified minimum annual revenue.

B: Entrepreneurs: Entrepreneurs must be partners in a company registered in the UAE under the SME category and have a minimum annual revenue of AED 1 million. This category aims to attract individuals who are actively involved in growing and developing businesses in the UAE.

C: Specialized Talents: Specialized talents, including doctors, scientists, artists, and researchers, must demonstrate exceptional skills and qualifications in their respective fields. They may also need to provide evidence of their achievements and contributions to their field to qualify for the Golden Visa.

D: Students: Students who wish to apply for the Golden Visa must have a certain level of academic achievement and be enrolled in a recognized educational institution in the UAE. They may also need to provide proof of their enrollment and academic standing to qualify for the visa.

Overall, the Golden Visa program in the UAE is designed to attract individuals who can contribute to the country's economy and society. By offering long-term residency permits to eligible individuals, the program aims to provide stability and security to visa holders and their families, while also stimulating economic growth and innovation in the UAE.

II: Specific Requirements for Investors, Entrepreneurs, Specialized Talents, Students, and Researchers

A: Investors: To qualify for the Golden Visa as an investor, individuals must have a minimum investment of AED 2 million in the UAE. This investment can be in the form of investment funds, commercial or industrial investments, or ownership of a company with a specified minimum annual revenue. Investors must also provide proof of their investment and its impact on the UAE economy.

B: Entrepreneurs: Entrepreneurs must be partners in a company registered in the UAE under the SME category and have a minimum annual revenue of AED 1 million. They must also demonstrate that their business is contributing to the growth and development of the UAE economy.

C: Specialized Talents: Specialized talents, such as doctors, scientists, artists, and researchers, must demonstrate exceptional skills and qualifications in their respective fields. They may also need to provide evidence of their achievements and contributions to their field, such as publications, patents, or awards.

D: Students: Students who wish to apply for the Golden Visa must have a certain level of academic achievement and be enrolled in a recognized educational institution in the UAE. They may also need to provide proof of their enrollment and academic standing, such as transcripts or letters of recommendation.

E: Researchers: Researchers must have specific achievements and strong influence in their fields, recommended by the Emirates Scientists Council. They may also need to provide evidence of their research contributions and publications.

Overall, the specific requirements for each category of the Golden Visa program are designed to ensure that individuals who qualify for the visa can contribute to the UAE's economy and society. By attracting high net worth individuals, investors, entrepreneurs, specialized talents, students, and researchers, the Golden Visa program aims to promote innovation, economic growth, and cultural exchange in the UAE.

III: Criteria for Renewal and Extension of the Golden Visa

The Golden Visa is initially valid for 5-10 years, depending on the category of the applicant. To renew or extend the visa, individuals must continue to meet the eligibility criteria and requirements set forth by the UAE government. This may include maintaining the minimum investment for investors, demonstrating continued professional achievements for specialized talents, and maintaining a certain level of academic performance for students.

A: Investors: To renew or extend the Golden Visa as an investor, individuals must continue to maintain their investment of AED 2 million in the UAE. They may also need to provide evidence of the impact of their investment on the UAE economy and their continued involvement in their investment activities.

B: Entrepreneurs: Entrepreneurs must continue to be partners in a company registered in the UAE under the SME category and maintain a minimum annual revenue of AED 1 million to renew or extend their Golden Visa. They may also need to demonstrate the growth and development of their business since obtaining the visa.

C: Specialized Talents: Specialized talents must continue to demonstrate exceptional skills and qualifications in their respective fields to renew or extend their Golden Visa. They may need to provide evidence of their continued professional achievements, such as publications, patents, or awards.

D: Students: Students must continue to maintain a certain level of academic achievement and be enrolled in a recognized educational institution in the UAE to renew or extend their Golden Visa. They may also need to provide proof of their continued enrollment and academic standing.

Overall, the criteria for renewal and extension of the Golden Visa are designed to ensure that individuals who hold the visa continue to contribute to the UAE's economy and society. By maintaining the eligibility criteria and requirements, the UAE government aims to attract and retain high net worth individuals, investors, entrepreneurs, specialized talents, students, and researchers in the country, promoting long-term economic growth and development.

Chapter 4

Benefits of the Golden Visa

I: 5-10 Years of Long-Term Residency in the UAE

One of the primary benefits of the Golden Visa is the long-term residency it offers in the UAE. Golden Visa holders are granted residency permits that are valid for 5-10 years, depending on the category of the applicant. This provides individuals and their families with stability and security, allowing them to live and work in the UAE for an extended period without the need for frequent renewals.

A: Stability and Security: The long-term residency offered by the Golden Visa provides individuals and their families with stability and security. They can plan their lives and futures in the UAE without the uncertainty of short-term visas.

B: Flexibility: Golden Visa holders have the flexibility to live and work in the UAE for an extended period without the need for frequent renewals. This allows them to focus on their professional and personal endeavors without the administrative burden of visa renewals.

C: Access to Services: Golden Visa holders have access to a range of services and benefits in the UAE, including healthcare, education, and employment opportunities. They can fully integrate into the UAE society and contribute to its economy and culture.

D: Family Reunification: The long-term residency offered by the Golden Visa allows families to stay together in the UAE. Golden Visa holders can sponsor their spouses, children, and parents, as well as domestic workers, to join them in the country.

E: Investment Opportunities: The long-term residency offered by the Golden Visa is also beneficial for investors and entrepreneurs. It allows them to oversee their investments and businesses in the UAE without the restrictions of short-term visas.

Overall, the long-term residency offered by the Golden Visa is a key benefit that attracts high net worth individuals, investors, entrepreneurs, specialized talents, students, and researchers to the UAE. It provides stability, security, and opportunities for growth and development, making the UAE an attractive destination for individuals seeking a prosperous future.

II: Ability to Live, Work, and Study in the UAE Without the Need for a National Sponsor

Unlike other residency programs in the UAE, the Golden Visa does not require individuals to have a national sponsor, also known as a "kafil." This means that Golden Visa holders have the freedom to live, work, and study in the UAE without the need for a local sponsor. This offers greater flexibility and independence, making it easier for individuals to pursue their professional and personal goals in the country.

A: Professional Freedom: Golden Visa holders have the freedom to work in any sector or profession in the UAE without the need for a local sponsor. This allows them to explore new career opportunities and advance their careers without restrictions.

B: Educational Opportunities: Golden Visa holders have access to a wide range of educational opportunities in the UAE, including universities, colleges, and vocational training institutes. They can pursue further education and skills development without the need for a local sponsor.

C: Business Ventures: Golden Visa holders can start their own businesses in the UAE without the need for a local sponsor. This allows them to pursue entrepreneurial ventures and contribute to the UAE's economy and business landscape.

D: Family Sponsorship: Golden Visa holders have the ability to sponsor their family members, including spouses, children, and parents, to join them in the UAE. This provides families with the opportunity to stay together and enjoy the benefits of living in the UAE.

E: Independence and Autonomy: The ability to live, work, and study in the UAE without the need for a national sponsor gives Golden Visa holders a sense of independence and autonomy. They can make their own decisions and pursue their goals without external interference.

Overall, the ability to live, work, and study in the UAE without the need for a national sponsor is a key benefit of the Golden Visa program. It offers individuals greater freedom and flexibility, making the UAE an attractive destination for those seeking a vibrant and dynamic environment to pursue their ambitions.

III: Free Travel and Special Discounts on Various Services and Amenities

Golden Visa holders enjoy several benefits when it comes to travel and lifestyle in the UAE. They are entitled to free travel to and from the UAE, making it convenient for them to visit family and friends or travel for business or leisure purposes. Additionally, Golden Visa holders are eligible for special discounts on various services and amenities in the UAE, including car rentals, hotels, restaurants, and entertainment venues. These discounts can help reduce the cost of living in the UAE and enhance the overall quality of life for Golden Visa holders and their families.

A: Free Travel: Golden Visa holders can enjoy free travel to and from the UAE, eliminating the need to purchase expensive flight tickets. This can save them a significant amount of money and make it easier for them to travel for personal or business reasons.

B: Discounts on Services: Golden Visa holders are eligible for special discounts on various services in the UAE, including car rentals, hotels, restaurants, and entertainment venues. These discounts can help Golden Visa holders save money on their everyday expenses and enjoy a higher standard of living in the UAE.

C: Quality of Life: The benefits of free travel and special discounts on services and amenities can enhance the overall quality of life for Golden Visa holders and their families. They can enjoy a wide range of leisure activities and experiences in the UAE, making their time in the country more enjoyable and fulfilling.

D: Economic Impact: The free travel and special discounts offered to Golden Visa holders can also have a positive economic impact on the UAE. By encouraging Golden Visa holders to spend money on goods and services in the country, these benefits can help stimulate economic growth and create new job opportunities for UAE residents.

Overall, the free travel and special discounts offered to Golden Visa holders make the UAE a more attractive destination for high net worth individuals, investors, entrepreneurs, specialized talents, students, and researchers. These benefits can enhance the overall experience of living in the UAE and contribute to the country's reputation as a global hub for business, tourism, and innovation.

IV: Enhanced Security and Peace of Mind for the Future

Perhaps one of the most significant benefits of the Golden Visa is the enhanced security and peace of mind it offers for the future. By obtaining a Golden Visa, individuals and their families can secure their residency in the UAE for an extended period, providing them with stability and security in a rapidly changing world. This can be especially valuable for individuals who are looking to establish roots in the UAE and build a successful future for themselves and their families.

A: Stability and Continuity: The Golden Visa offers stability and continuity for individuals and their families, allowing them to plan for the future with confidence. Knowing that they have long-term residency in the UAE can provide peace of mind and security, especially in uncertain times.

B: Investment in the Future: For investors and entrepreneurs, the Golden Visa represents an investment in the future of their business and their family. It allows them to focus on growing their business and contributing to the UAE's economy without worrying about their residency status.

C: Family Security: The Golden Visa allows families to stay together in the UAE, providing a sense of security and stability for everyone. Families can build a life in the UAE knowing that they have the right to reside in the country for an extended period.

D: Professional Development: For specialized talents, researchers, and students, the Golden Visa provides an opportunity for professional development and academic growth in the UAE. It allows them to pursue their passions and contribute to their fields without the constraints of short-term visas.

E: Global Mobility: The Golden Visa also offers global mobility, allowing individuals to travel freely to and from the UAE. This can be beneficial for business travel, family visits, and leisure trips, enhancing the overall quality of life for Golden Visa holders and their families.

In conclusion, the Golden Visa program in the UAE offers a range of benefits for individuals seeking to live and work in the country. From long-term residency to freedom from national sponsorship, free travel, and discounts on services, the Golden Visa provides a pathway to a stable and prosperous future in the UAE.

Chapter 5

Impact on Business and Investment

I: How the Golden Visa Program has Attracted Investors and Entrepreneurs to the UAE

The Golden Visa program in the UAE has been instrumental in attracting investors and entrepreneurs from around the world. The program offers long-term residency permits to individuals who meet certain investment criteria, providing them with the stability and security needed to establish and grow their businesses in the UAE.

A: Business-Friendly Environment: One of the key factors that has made the Golden Visa program attractive to investors and entrepreneurs is the business-friendly environment of the UAE. With its strategic location, modern infrastructure, and favorable tax policies, the UAE offers a wealth of opportunities for businesses looking to expand or relocate.

B: Investment Opportunities: The Golden Visa program has opened up new investment opportunities for individuals looking to invest in the UAE. By offering long-term residency permits, the program provides investors with the confidence and security needed to commit to long-term investments in the country.

C: Reputation as a Global Hub: Additionally, the Golden Visa program has helped to enhance the UAE's reputation as a global hub for business and innovation. By attracting top talent and investment, the program has helped to stimulate economic growth and create new job opportunities in the country.

D: Stimulating Economic Growth: The influx of investors and entrepreneurs through the Golden Visa program has had a positive impact on the UAE's economy. It has led to the creation of new businesses, increased employment opportunities, and a boost in economic activity in various sectors.

E: Enhancing Innovation: The Golden Visa program has also contributed to the enhancement of innovation in the UAE. By attracting talented individuals and entrepreneurs, the program has encouraged the development of new ideas, technologies, and solutions that have benefited the country's economy and society as a whole.

Overall, the Golden Visa program has been highly successful in attracting investors and entrepreneurs to the UAE. Its benefits extend beyond the individuals who directly benefit from the program, contributing to the overall growth and development of the country's economy and business landscape.

II: Case Studies of Successful Businesses and Projects Initiated by Golden Visa Holders

There are numerous examples of successful businesses and projects that have been initiated by Golden Visa holders in the UAE. For example, many investors have established successful real estate developments, hotels, and restaurants in the country, contributing to the growth of the tourism and hospitality sectors.

1: Real Estate Developments: Golden Visa holders have played a significant role in the development of the UAE's real estate sector. Many investors have launched successful residential and commercial projects, including luxury hotels, shopping malls, and office buildings. These developments have not only contributed to the country's economy but have also enhanced its reputation as a global business and leisure destination.

2: Hospitality Sector: The hospitality sector in the UAE has also benefited from the presence of Golden Visa holders. Many investors have opened hotels and resorts, catering to the growing number of tourists and business travelers visiting the country. These establishments have not only created jobs but have also contributed to the overall growth and development of the hospitality industry in the UAE.

3: Startups and Technology Companies: Entrepreneurs holding Golden Visas have launched innovative startups and technology companies in the UAE, taking advantage of the country's advanced infrastructure and supportive business environment. These companies have introduced new technologies and services, driving innovation and growth in the UAE's tech sector.

4: Economic Impact: The businesses and projects initiated by Golden Visa holders have had a significant economic impact on the UAE. They have created jobs, driven economic growth, and contributed to the diversification of the country's economy away from oil dependence.

5: Positioning the UAE as a Leader: The success of these businesses and projects has helped to position the UAE as a leader in various industries, including real estate, hospitality, and technology. The country's reputation as a business-friendly destination has been further enhanced, attracting more investors and entrepreneurs to the UAE.

Overall, the businesses and projects initiated by Golden Visa holders have had a positive impact on the UAE's economy and business landscape. They have contributed to the country's growth and development, showcasing the benefits of the Golden Visa program for both individuals and the UAE as a whole.

III: Economic Impact and Contribution to the UAE's GDP

The Golden Visa program has had a significant impact on the UAE's economy, contributing to its GDP growth and economic diversification. By attracting foreign investment and top talent, the program has helped to stimulate growth in key sectors such as real estate, tourism, and technology.

A: Foreign Direct Investment (FDI): The Golden Visa program has attracted a substantial amount of foreign direct investment (FDI) into the UAE. Investors seeking the benefits of the Golden Visa have invested in various sectors of the economy, including real estate, hospitality, and technology. This influx of investment has contributed to the growth of these sectors and has helped to diversify the UAE's economy away from its traditional reliance on oil.

B: Job Creation: The program has also led to the creation of new job opportunities for UAE nationals and expatriates. As businesses initiated by Golden Visa holders expand, they require a workforce to support their operations. This has helped to drive down unemployment rates in the country and has improved the overall standard of living for residents.

C: Economic Diversification: The Golden Visa program has played a crucial role in the UAE's efforts to diversify its economy. By attracting investors and entrepreneurs from diverse industries, the program has helped to stimulate growth in non-oil sectors, reducing the country's dependence on oil revenue.

D: Innovation and Technology: The program has also contributed to the development of the UAE's innovation and technology sector. Entrepreneurs and startups initiated by Golden Visa holders have introduced new technologies and services, driving innovation and growth in the country's tech sector.

E: Future Growth: As the Golden Visa program continues to evolve and expand, its impact on the UAE's economy is expected to grow even further. The program has positioned the UAE as a global leader in business and innovation, attracting top talent and investment from around the world.

Overall, the Golden Visa program has been a key driver of economic growth and development in the UAE. Its contribution to the country's GDP growth, job creation, and economic diversification highlights its importance as a catalyst for change in the country's economy.

Chapter 6

Cultural and Social Integration

I: Importance of Cultural Diversity and Inclusivity in the UAE

The United Arab Emirates (UAE) is known for its rich cultural heritage and diversity, with people from various backgrounds and nationalities living and working together harmoniously. Cultural diversity is seen as a source of strength in the UAE, contributing to the country's vibrant social fabric and economic prosperity.

A: Cultural Heritage: The UAE's cultural diversity is rooted in its history as a trading hub, where people from different parts of the world came together to exchange goods and ideas. This has created a unique blend of cultures, traditions, and languages that is evident in the country's cuisine, architecture, and art.

B: Economic Prosperity: Cultural diversity has played a significant role in the UAE's economic prosperity. The presence of a diverse workforce has allowed the country to tap into a wide range of skills and talents, driving innovation and growth in key sectors such as finance, tourism, and technology.

C: Social Fabric: Inclusivity is a key value in the UAE, with the government and society at large working to ensure that all individuals, regardless of their background, feel welcome and valued in the country. This commitment to inclusivity has helped to create a sense of unity and cohesion among the diverse population of the UAE.

D: Cultural Exchange: The UAE actively promotes cultural exchange and understanding through various initiatives and events. The country's cultural festivals, museums, and art galleries showcase its rich heritage and provide opportunities for people from different backgrounds to come together and learn from one another.

E: Global Perspective: The UAE's cultural diversity has also helped to shape its global perspective. The country's leaders are committed to fostering international cooperation and understanding, and this is reflected in its foreign policy and diplomatic efforts.

Overall, cultural diversity and inclusivity are core values in the UAE, contributing to its identity as a modern, progressive, and welcoming society.

II: Initiatives to Promote Cultural Exchange and Understanding Among Golden Visa Holders and Local Communities

The UAE government has launched several initiatives to promote cultural exchange and understanding among Golden Visa holders and local communities. These initiatives aim to celebrate the country's cultural diversity and heritage while fostering a sense of unity and cohesion among its residents. Some of the key initiatives include:

A: Cultural Festivals: The UAE hosts a variety of cultural festivals throughout the year, showcasing the music, dance, food, and traditions of different communities. These festivals provide an opportunity for Golden Visa holders and local residents to experience and learn about other cultures.

B: Art Exhibitions: The UAE is home to many art galleries and museums that showcase both traditional and contemporary art from around the world. These exhibitions help to promote cross-cultural dialogue and understanding among Golden Visa holders and local communities.

C: Heritage Tours: The UAE's rich history and heritage are showcased through heritage tours that take visitors to historical sites, museums, and cultural landmarks. These tours provide insights into the country's past and its cultural identity.

D: Language and Cultural Exchange Programs: The UAE offers language and cultural exchange programs that allow Golden Visa holders to learn about Emirati culture and traditions while sharing their own culture with local communities. These programs help to break down cultural barriers and promote mutual understanding.

E: Community Engagement Activities: The UAE government encourages Golden Visa holders to participate in community engagement activities such as volunteering, charity events, and social initiatives. These activities help to build bridges between different communities and foster a sense of belonging and solidarity.

Overall, these initiatives play a crucial role in promoting cultural exchange and understanding among Golden Visa holders and local communities in the UAE. They help to celebrate diversity, promote inclusivity, and build a more harmonious and cohesive society.

III: Impact on Societal Values and Norms

The Golden Visa program has had a profound impact on societal values and norms in the UAE, promoting tolerance, diversity, and inclusivity. By bringing together people from different backgrounds and nationalities, the program has helped to break down barriers and stereotypes, fostering a more open and accepting society.

A: Tolerance and Diversity: The UAE has long been known for its welcoming attitude towards people of all backgrounds, and the Golden Visa program has further promoted this culture of tolerance and diversity. Golden Visa holders contribute to the country's cultural tapestry, enriching the local community with their unique perspectives and traditions.

B: Innovation and Entrepreneurship: The program has also helped to promote a culture of innovation and entrepreneurship in the UAE. Many Golden Visa holders are highly skilled professionals and entrepreneurs who bring new ideas and technologies to the country, contributing to its economic growth and development.

C: Cultural Exchange: The program has facilitated greater cultural exchange and understanding among residents of the UAE. Golden Visa holders have the opportunity to share their own cultures and traditions with the local community, while also learning about Emirati culture and values.

D: Economic Growth: The presence of Golden Visa holders has had a positive impact on the UAE's economy, contributing to its diversification and growth. Their contributions to various sectors of the economy, such as real estate, tourism, and technology, have helped to create jobs and drive economic development.

E: Social Integration: The program has played a role in promoting social integration in the UAE. Golden Visa holders are encouraged to participate in community activities and events, helping to bridge the gap between different communities and foster a sense of unity and belonging.

Overall, the Golden Visa program has had a transformative impact on societal values and norms in the UAE, promoting tolerance, diversity, and inclusivity. As the program continues to evolve, its positive impact on the country's cultural landscape is expected to grow, further enriching the fabric of Emirati society.

Chapter 7
Future Prospects and Challenges

I: Potential Growth Areas and Opportunities for Further Development of the Golden Visa Program

Despite its many benefits, the Golden Visa program in the UAE also faces several challenges. These challenges include:

A: Competition from Other Countries: The UAE faces stiff competition from other countries that offer similar residency programs for investors and skilled professionals. Countries like the United States, Canada, and Australia offer attractive residency programs that compete with the UAE's Golden Visa program.

B: Changing Economic Conditions: The economic conditions in the UAE and around the world can impact the attractiveness of the Golden Visa program. Economic downturns or changes in government policies can affect the demand for residency in the UAE.

C: Regulatory Changes: Changes in government regulations and policies can also impact the Golden Visa program. For example, changes to the eligibility criteria or investment requirements could affect the program's appeal to potential applicants.

D: Integration and Social Cohesion: While the Golden Visa program has helped to promote cultural exchange and understanding, integrating a large number of expatriates into Emirati society can present challenges. Ensuring social cohesion and harmony among diverse communities is an ongoing challenge for the UAE government.

E: Sustainability and Long-Term Impact: Ensuring the long-term sustainability and impact of the Golden Visa program is also a challenge. The program must continue to evolve and adapt to changing economic, social, and political conditions to remain relevant and effective.

Overall, while the Golden Visa program in the UAE has been successful in attracting talent and investment to the country, it also faces several challenges that must be addressed to ensure its continued success.

II: Challenges Faced by Golden Visa Holders and the UAE Government

To enhance the effectiveness and sustainability of the Golden Visa program, the UAE government can consider the following strategies:

A: Continuous Evaluation and Improvement: The government should continuously evaluate the Golden Visa program and make improvements based on feedback from stakeholders. This could include streamlining the application process, updating eligibility criteria, and expanding the program to include new categories of beneficiaries.

B: Promoting Awareness and Understanding: The government should continue to promote awareness and understanding of the Golden Visa program among potential applicants, both domestically and internationally. This could include marketing campaigns, informational seminars, and partnerships with relevant organizations.

C: Enhancing Integration and Social Cohesion: The government should take steps to enhance the integration of Golden Visa holders into Emirati society and promote social cohesion among diverse communities. This could include initiatives to foster cultural exchange, promote tolerance and understanding, and provide support services for Golden Visa holders and their families.

D: Strengthening Regulatory Framework: The government should strengthen the regulatory framework governing the Golden Visa program to ensure compliance with the terms and conditions of the visas. This could include stricter enforcement measures and penalties for non-compliance.

E: Monitoring Economic and Social Impact: The government should closely monitor the economic and social impact of the Golden Visa program to ensure that it is achieving its intended objectives. This could include conducting regular evaluations and surveys to assess the program's impact on the economy, society, and the overall well-being of the country.

By implementing these strategies, the UAE government can enhance the effectiveness and sustainability of the Golden Visa program, ensuring that it continues to attract top talent and investment to the country for years to come.

III: Strategies to Enhance the Program's Effectiveness and Sustainability

A: Streamline Application Process: Simplify and expedite the application process to attract more high-quality applicants. Reducing bureaucratic hurdles can make the program more attractive and competitive globally.

B: Enhance Support Services: Provide comprehensive support services to Golden Visa holders, including access to healthcare, education, and housing. This can improve the quality of life for visa holders and their families, encouraging them to stay longer in the UAE.

C: Promote Cultural Integration: Implement programs that promote cultural integration between Golden Visa holders and the local community. This can help build a more inclusive and cohesive society.

D: Regular Evaluation and Improvement: Continuously evaluate the program's performance and make improvements based on feedback. This can help address any issues or challenges that arise and ensure the program remains relevant and effective.

E: Expand Eligibility Criteria: Consider expanding the eligibility criteria to include new categories of beneficiaries, such as artists, athletes, and cultural icons. This can attract individuals with exceptional talent and achievements, enriching the cultural landscape of the UAE.

By implementing these strategies, the UAE can enhance the effectiveness and sustainability of the Golden Visa program, ensuring that it continues to attract top talent and investment to the country.

Conclusion

The UAE Golden Visa program has emerged as a beacon of opportunity, attracting talented individuals and investors from around the world. Since its inception in 2019, the program has witnessed significant growth, with around 80,000 Golden Visas issued in 2022 alone. This surge in interest is a testament to the program's success in attracting top talent and investment to the UAE.

One of the key strengths of the Golden Visa program is its ability to provide long-term stability and security to individuals and their families. By offering residency permits valid for 5-10 years, the program gives Golden Visa holders the freedom to live, work, and study in the UAE without the need for frequent renewals or a national sponsor. This has made the UAE an attractive destination for individuals seeking a stable and prosperous future.

The Golden Visa program has also had a positive impact on business and investment in the UAE. By attracting investors and entrepreneurs from around the world, the program has helped to stimulate economic growth and create new job opportunities in the country. Additionally, the program has contributed to the UAE's reputation as a global hub for business and innovation, positioning the country as a leader in various industries.

Looking ahead, it is essential to nurture and evolve the Golden Visa program to ensure its long-term success and benefits for all stakeholders involved. This includes enhancing the program's effectiveness and sustainability, addressing any challenges faced by Golden Visa holders and the UAE government, and continuing to promote cultural exchange and understanding among Golden Visa holders and local communities.

Overall, the UAE Golden Visa program has been a resounding success, attracting top talent and investment to the country and shaping its future as a global leader. By continuing to support and develop the program, the UAE can build on its success and further enhance its position as a dynamic and thriving destination for individuals and businesses alike.

www.ingramcontent.com/pod-product-compliance
Lightning Source LLC
Chambersburg PA
CBHW070950220526
45471CB00007B/2966